SOFTBALL

SOFTBALL: POSITIONS

BARBARA BONNEY

The Rourke Corporation, Inc.
Vero Beach, Florida 32964

Barbara Bonney is a librarian and freelance writer in Cincinnati, Ohio. Besides enjoying research and words, she likes creating with food and fabrics. She has two children.

PHOTO CREDITS:
All photos © Tony Gray except; © East Coast Studios: page 7, 19, 21, 22

EDITORIAL SERVICES:
Susan Albury

Library of Congress Cataloging-in-Publication Data

Bonney, Barbara, 1955-
   Softball—positions / by Barbara Bonney.
     p. cm. — (Softball)
   Includes index
   Summary: Briefly describes each of the positions on a softball team and offers advice on playing these positions.
   ISBN 0-86593-479-7
   1. Softball—Juvenile literature. 2. Softball players—Juvenile literature.
[1. Softball.] I. Title. II. Series: Bonney, Barbara, 1955- Softball.
GV881.15.B65 1998
796.357'8—dc21
                                          98–11084
                                            CIP
                                            AC

Printed in the USA

TABLE OF CONTENTS

PITCHER

It may seem like all the pitcher does is throw the ball, but that is not true. A pitcher also covers first base when needed and backs up action at home plate. A pitcher **fields** (FEELDZ) **bunts** (BUNTZ) and backs up throws made from outfield to second and third bases. When a ball is hit hard up the middle of the field, the pitcher must be ready to catch it. The most important job of the pitcher in a fast-pitch game, though, is to throw **strikes** (STRYKZ) and to keep calm during the game. A pitcher must be smart and make good decisions.

When a ball is hit between an outfielder and infielder, the outfielder has first chance to get it.

Pitching is just one responsibility of the pitcher.

CATCHER

The catcher's most important job is to catch pitches, but it is not the only duty. Others include catching **pop-ups** (POP-ups), backing up first base, and **tagging** (TAG ing) runners at home plate. Catchers have a squatting stance behind the batter, but when the ball is hit, they must be able to rush into action.

A squatting stance behind home plate makes the catcher able to jump up quickly if needed.

A fast-pitch catcher wears a lot of protective equipment.

It is the catcher who figures out the weaknesses of the batters and signals teammates how to play for those weaknesses. Because of all of these skills, a catcher must be **agile** (AJ ul), have a strong and accurate overhand throw, be a leader, stay alert, and be able to take a few bumps from runners at home plate. In fast-pitch softball, catchers must wear a mask, helmet, chest protector, and shin guards.

INFIELDERS

Infielders are the players who **defend** (dee FEND) the area of the field around the bases. They must always be ready and alert. If the ball comes their way and they do not know immediately where to throw it, seconds are lost. Those seconds could be an advantage for the other team. To be ready, the infielders should know how many outs there are, what the score is, and places where the ball may need to be thrown. Then when the ball comes to an infielder, catching and throwing become one smooth motion and the **play** (PLAY) is made.

Infielders guard the bases and stay alert.

FIRST BASE

A player covering first base should have excellent catching skills. A tall player can be a larger target for throws coming to first base and height can also help when a player needs to stretch to catch a ball. A left-handed player has a natural reach toward second base which fills a fielding gap and keeps him or her out of the runner's way. First base players need to be able to run quickly to catch foul balls and might also cover home plate. Having good balance and footwork can help the player make the plays.

Each position has a lot of ground to defend so that the whole infield and outfield is covered.

This first base player waits for the ball with her foot touching the base.

11

SECOND BASE

Players in this position must be able to do a little bit of everything. Fielding is important, but so is speed and throwing skills.

Second base players need to watch the action and know what to do when they get the ball.

Working with others is important for a second base player.

A second base player might cover pop-ups, bunts, and ground balls in a large area. This person needs to be alert and know what to do with the ball when it comes. Working with the shortstop and first base player is important.

THIRD BASE

Many beginning players bat right-handed and hit balls toward third base. The player defending third base must be able to catch these hits whether they are grounders, line drives, or pop-ups. If the hits get past the third baseman, the ball can roll a good distance before an outfielder can be there to back up. A good third base player will also rush in to field bunts. Because of the greater distance between third base and first base, the player at third base must have a strong arm and accurate aim.

Knowing and playing positions well makes a team work smoothly.

Third base gets a lot of action and the third base player must be prepared.

SHORTSTOP

A shortstop does not have a base to cover, except as a backup for second and third bases. The shortstop has to cover a wide area, though, from second base to third and parts of both the infield and outfield. The shortstop should be an excellent fielder but also be able to make the long throw to first base. When outfielders need to **relay** (REE lay) the ball to the infield, often the ball is thrown to the shortstop. A fast thinker and quick mover makes a good shortstop since the position changes with each situation.

This shortstop is ready to run, catch, and throw to get the other team out.

OUTFIELDERS

Outfielders are the last line of defense in the field. A ball that has traveled that far is a good hit and mistakes can cost the defense much more than they do in the infield. However, beginning softball players do not often hit the ball to the outfield and so the outfield players do not see a lot of action.

Playing outfield requires a positive attitude and paying attention to the game.

After running quickly to get the ball, outfielders need a strong arm to throw it to the infield.

The hardest job of an outfielder is to stay alert and be prepared. Knowing the score, the count, and the way each batter hits can help the outfielders be ready. When the fly ball comes, the outfielder must run quickly to be in position under the ball and stretch their arm above the head for the catch. Outfielders must have good throwing arms to relay the ball to the infield. In fast-pitch, there are three outfield positions: right, center, and left. In slow-pitch, a fourth, short outfield, is added.

SHIFTING POSITIONS

Even though softball is played with positions and each position has a job to do, no player should just stand in position and wait for a play to happen. As soon as the ball is hit, all players should move. Some move in on the ball, others back up. Some see what might happen next and get prepared. Team players play their position but shift to help each other without getting in the way. Team members can help by covering bases or backing up positions.

Calling "Mine!" or "I have it!" is smart when more than one player is trying to catch the ball. Yell loud enough for the other players to hear.

As the ball is hit, players move to fill gaps and back up other players.

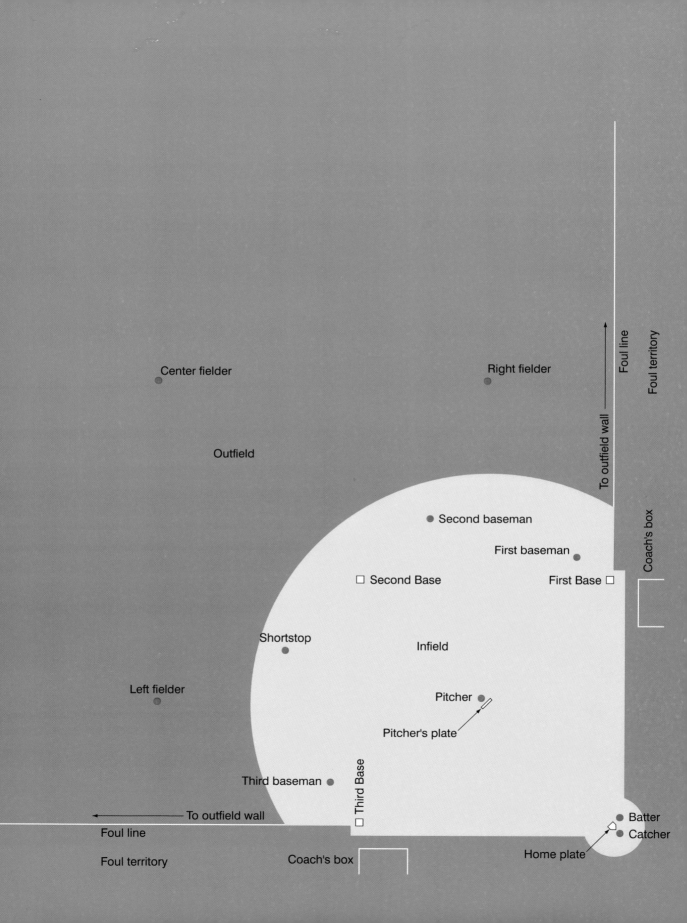

GLOSSARY

agile (AJ ul) — able to move quickly

bunt (BUNT) — a hit where the ball is batted softly on purpose

defend (dee FEND) — to protect

field (FEELD) — getting the ball by catching or picking it up after it has been hit

play (PLAY) — a move or set of moves in a game

pop-ups (POP-ups) — a short, high fly ball that is easily caught

relay (REE lay) — returning the ball in short fast throws between several players rather than throwing the ball a very long distance

strike (STRYK) — a pitch that is swung at and missed or hit into foul territory; also a pitch thrown into the strike zone and not swung at

tagging (TAG ing) — putting the runner out by touching him/her with the ball or with the hand holding the ball

Softball positions begin at the points on the diagram but move a lot during plays.

INDEX

FURTHER READING

Find out more about softball with these helpful books and information sites:

Elliott, Jill & Martha Ewing, eds. *Youth Softball: A Complete Handbook.* printed by Brown & Benchmark, 1992

Rookie Coaches Softball Guide/American Sport Education Program. Human Kinetics Publishers, Inc., 1992

Cohen, Neil, ed. *The Everything You Wanted to Know About Sports Encyclopedia.* Bantam Books, 1994

Boehm, David A., editor-in-chief. *Guinness Sports Record Book 1990-91.* Sterling Publishing Co., Inc. 1990

on the internet at
www.softball.com/othrlink.htm (links to organizations, equipment manufacturers, teams, etc)